EARTH

FEELING THE HEAT

To everyone, everywhere, taking action
to help our earth —B. Z. G.

To my classmates and faculty at
FIT Masters of Illustration Program, 2007 —C. W.

With thanks to Laura Godwin, Noa Wheeler, and April Ward
for such inspired and creative work on this book

Henry Holt and Company, LLC, *Publishers since 1866*
175 Fifth Avenue, New York, New York 10010
www.HenryHoltKids.com

Library of Congress Cataloging-in-Publication Data
Guiberson, Brenda Z.
Earth: feeling the heat / Brenda Z. Guiberson ; illustrated by Chad Wallace. — 1st ed.
p.   cm.
ISBN 978-0-8050-7719-3
1. Global warming—Juvenile literature. 2. Global temperature changes—
Juvenile literature. I. Wallace, Chad, ill. II. Title.
QC981.8.G56G85 2010   577.27'6—dc22   2009012219

First Edition—2010 / Designed by April Ward
Printed in October 2009 in China by SNP Leefung Printers Ltd.,
Dongguan City, Guangdong Province, on acid-free paper. ∞

1 3 5 7 9 10 8 6 4 2

FEELING THE HEAT

BRENDA Z. GUIBERSON

ILLUSTRATED BY CHAD WALLACE

HENRY HOLT AND COMPANY | NEW YORK

In the Canadian Arctic, a polar bear shuffles across the ice, hunting for seals. But the frozen sea is melting fast. *Dripdripdrip.* The ice tips, the bear topples, and the seal hunt ends far too early. Because the Arctic keeps getting warmer and warmer, the bear can't gain the weight she needs to raise a cub.

Who can help the

POLAR BEAR?

A puffin returns to nest on a rocky Scottish island. *Flapflapflap!* She dives and dives for sand eels, but her beak remains empty. The North Sea has become too warm for the small fish. None of the nesting puffins can find food for themselves or their chicks.

Who can help the

PUFFIN?

On the Great Barrier Reef in Australia, an orange-spotted filefish searches for coral polyps to eat. *Swishswish!* A large section of coral reef looks like a bleached skeleton. The shallow water has been so warm that the coral polyps couldn't survive the heat.

Who can help the FILEFISH?

In the Ross Sea of Antarctica, an Adélie penguin is desperate to get around a colossal chunk of ice. *Splashcrash!* In the rising warmth, miles and miles of melting glacier are breaking off from the icy continent. A giant iceberg blocks the entire penguin colony from their nesting island.

Who can help the

PENGUIN?

An Edith's checkerspot butterfly flutters across a California prairie on a schedule that butterflies have followed for thousands of years. *Flitflitflit.* She lays eggs on a snapdragon leaf so the larvae will hatch on a perfect food. But the temperature is warmer now, and the plant blooms ten days early. It is already dried up when the hungry caterpillars hatch.

Who can help the
BUTTERFLY?

In Tanzania, a zebra looks for a cool sip of water. *Slurpslurp.* The elephants and baboons are also thirsty and the water hole is shrinking fast. The African grasslands are in the midst of an extreme drought, and the zebra glomps through squishy mud as the heat dries up the water. *Squishsquosh!*

Who can help the
ZEBRA?

In the Kalimantan forest of Borneo, an orangutan gobbles fruit and then snoozes in the shady branches of a tree. It has been extra warm, and a wildfire blazes quickly through the dried-out forest. *Crackle! Sizzzz!* The orangutan escapes the flames, but now he is hot and can't find food in familiar places.

Who can help the

ORANGUTAN?

In the South African desert of Succulent Karoo, a long-nosed fly sips sweet nectar from a flower. *Bzztbzzt!* As he picks up pollen and carries it to other plants, he becomes a pollinator and helps the plants to grow. But the climate is warmer now with less rain. Many plants have shriveled up, and there is no longer enough food for the pollinators.

Who can help the FLY?

In the rain forest of Colombia, pools of water are drying up before tadpoles have had a chance to mature. *Sloop!* With warmer nights, a fungus is flourishing in many places around the world and quickly kills frogs and toads. Because of the climate change, the golden toad has already become extinct. The bicolored dart frog is threatened and so are many other kinds of zip-zapping, insect-eating amphibians.

Who can help the

FROG?

Caribou search for lichen in an Alaskan forest. Spruce bark beetles are everywhere, chewing up the bark. *Chompchompchomp!* It is so much warmer here than usual that the beetles enjoy easy winters and a faster life cycle. Their exploding population has already killed forty million trees, and the caribou are hungry.

Who can help the

CARIBOU?

On a Himalayan mountain in Nepal, ancient glaciers are melting away. *Dribbledribbledrip.* A pika has a hard time keeping cool and finding enough grass to store for winter. As ice melts and the mountain gets warmer, alpine plants can grow only at higher and cooler elevations. The pika moves up, too, and so do the blue sheep and the snow leopard. When they reach the top, where else can they go?

Who can help the
PIKA?

In Bangladesh, the lowlands are covered with seawater. *Splishsplash.* A Bengal tiger swims along the coastline, looking for food. Two islands have already disappeared, and the mangrove forests are swamped. For miles around, creatures leave flooded areas and search for freshwater, food, and shelter. With a warming ocean and melting glaciers, the level of the sea keeps rising.

Who can help the **TIGER?**

A polar bear, a puffin, an orange-spotted filefish, an Adélie penguin, an Edith's checkerspot butterfly, a zebra, an orangutan, a long-nosed fly, a bicolored dart frog, a caribou, a pika, and even a Bengal tiger cannot stop the warming.

WHO CAN?

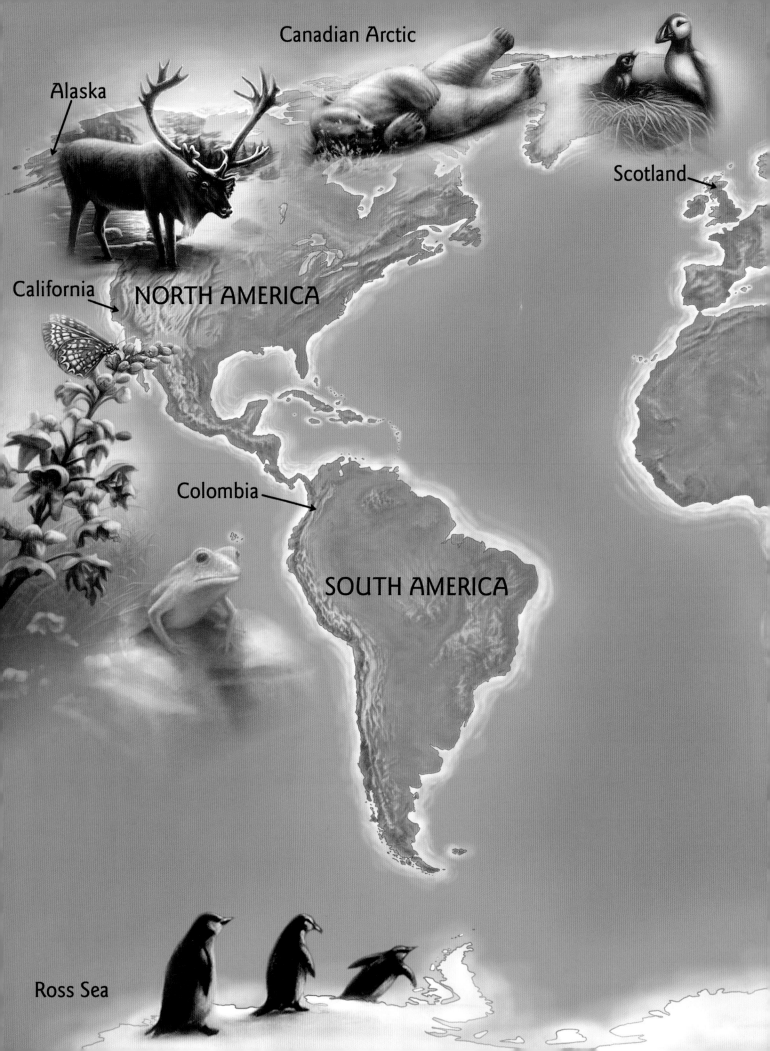

Canadian Arctic

Alaska

Scotland

California

NORTH AMERICA

Colombia

SOUTH AMERICA

Ross Sea

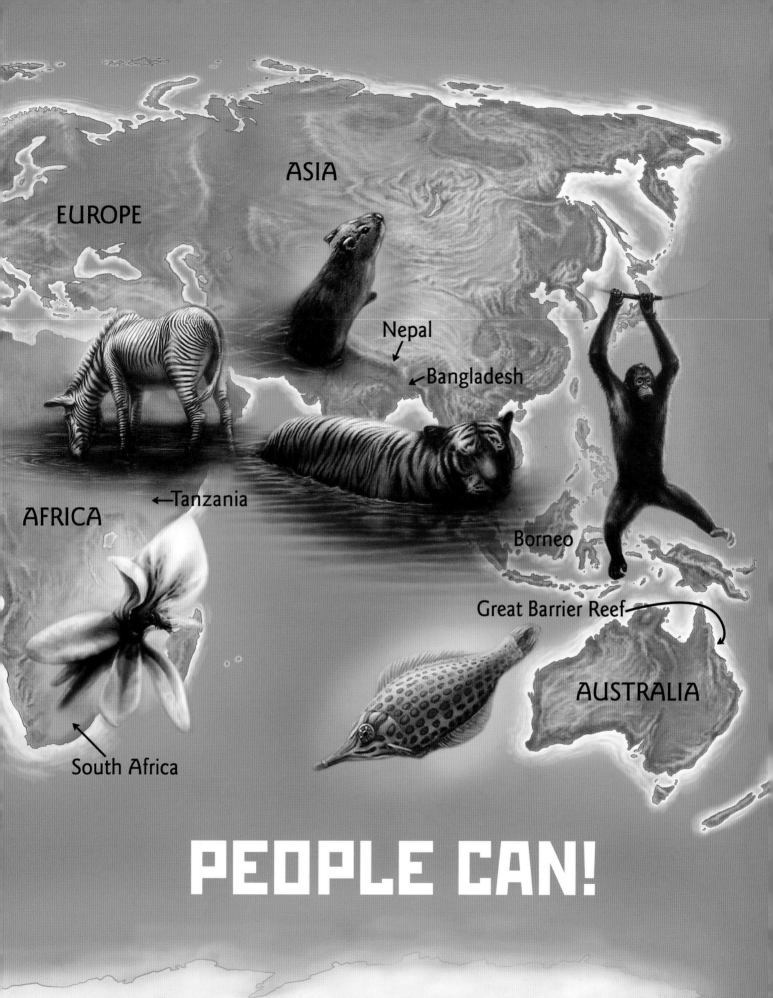

EUROPE

ASIA

AFRICA

AUSTRALIA

Nepal

Bangladesh

Tanzania

Borneo

Great Barrier Reef

South Africa

PEOPLE CAN!

ANTARCTICA

Let your hair air-dry and hang your laundry on a clothesline instead of using dryers.

Eat less meat. Raising animals, such as chickens and cows, uses more energy than growing plants.

Carry a reusable bag when shopping.

Recycle at home and school. Recycling takes less energy than making new products.

IN EVERY CORNER of the world, humans *zoom zoom* from here to there, push buttons, turn keys, and flip switches. With clever inventions, people fly like birds and keep warm like polar bears. But to do these things, humans burn oil, gas, and coal, all of which release particles into the air. These particles hover over the earth like a thick blanket that traps sunshine and makes everything extra warm. This is called global warming.

People and all the animals are feeling the heat. You can help by using less energy. Even the little things you do can make a big difference!

Don't turn up the heat when it's cold. Put on a sweater! Fleece clothing is extra warm and made from recycled plastic bottles.

Turn off lights and appliances when you leave a room.

Plant trees, especially those native to your area. Trees absorb carbon dioxide. A shady tree on the sunny side of the house cuts air-conditioning use by up to 16 percent.

Cut down on car trips. Walk, skateboard, bike, or carpool instead.

Take short showers and turn off the water while brushing your teeth.

Can you think of other ways to use less energy around your house and school?